Australians being Aussies

Presents

The New AUSSIE SLANG

Sayings and history

Created, compiled and written by
Shaun O'Brien

www.giddaymate.com.au

Shaun O'Brien

Shaun O'Brien
AUTHOR
(Proud Aussie, and all round good bloke)

My interest in Aussie slang really started when I was listening to talk back radio, you get to hear some amazing people and their stories.

Australian people are a resilient lot, we band together through floods, bush fires, cyclones and anything else that Mother Nature can throw at us. We are known as the lucky country, how is that? We live on one of the driest places on the planet; we have some of the deadliest spiders and some of the most venomous snakes. I reckon we are lucky because we are born of free spirit, it's our people and our characters that make's Australia, you and me, real Aussies....

Australia's beauty apart from the Great Barrier Reef, our Magnificent beaches, Kakadu, Tasmanian Wilderness just to name a few..Are our people..(Aussies).

Giddaymate was born out of an idea to discover the origin of Australian slang. Along the journey I researched the history of the Australian language, it's full of humour, back handed compliments, mateship and rhythmic disguises.

You know when you meet a real Aussie; they will greet you with a hearty Giddaymate, and a huge cheeky grin. They will ask you howzit goin.. good?, and before you know it they will be buying you a beer.. before talking your ear off about sport, politics or they will just rabbit on about whatever comes to their mind, most of it filled with humour and delivered with full enthusiasm.

So help us keep our slang alive, have a Captain Cook, it's a Cracker of a book…

Make someone's day and give them a laugh.
Good on ya. Hava good one and I'll catch ya ron….

Shaun

www.giddaymate.com.au

All rights reserved

This book or parts thereof may not be reproduced in any form without written permission from the author

Giddaymate Australia

ABN   44 557 260 707

email: shaun@giddaymate.com.au

www.giddaymate.com.au

Giddaymate was born out of an idea to discover the origin of Australian slang. Along the journey I researched the history of the Australian language. It is full of humour, back handed compliments, mateship, and rhythmic disguises. The uniqueness of the Aussie Slang is recognised worldwide, through our twang, shortening of words, and our tone, when we are delivering a phrase or saying.

I hope you, your mates, and your family get a laugh out of this book, as I did putting it together.
Thanks Shaun....

We have put together a range of products, using the Aussie sayings (lingo) on, Birthday Cards, stubbie coolers, coffee mugs, T-Shirts and a calendar.

www.giddaymate.com.au
For more info please contact - shaun@giddaymate.com.au

Britain arrives and brings its convicts

A number of European explorers sailed the coast of Australia, then known as New Holland, in the 17 th century. However it wasn't until 1770 that Captain James Cook chartered the east coast and claimed it for Britain. The new outpost was put to use as a penal colony and on 26 January 1788, the First Fleet of 11 ships carrying 1,500 people – half of them convicts – arrived in Sydney Harbour. Until penal transportation ended in 1868, 160,000 men and women came to Australia as convicts. The foundations of Australian English were in the prison system. Convicts wanted to disguise their language so that no one would know what they were talking about.

" No other class of society would use slang more readily or adapt it more expertly to their new environment; no other class would have a better flair for concocting new terms to fit in with their new conditions in life"

Sidney Baker (The Australian Language, 1945)

In 1869, *Marcus Clarke* described how locals devised language to 'convey a more full and humorous nature'

Please enjoy some of our aussie lingo

A bit rough around the edges

Not feeling in top shape

"Howja pull up this mornin Bluey?"

"Oh it was a big night,
I'm feelin a bit rough round the edges."

A bloody balls up

A Big Big mistake

"Hardly anyone's turned up on time,
and we are runnin behind,
its a bloody balls up!"

About as ugly as a hat full of arseholes

Particularly unattractive

"Wadda ya mean good lookin,
I reckon they're as ugly as a hat full of arseholes."

About as useful as tits on a bull   Not very helpful

"Davo's wrecked it, so I've gotta fix it again,
he's about as useful as tits on a bull."

About as welcome as a pork chop in Jerusalem

Not at all welcome

"I dunno bout you guys, but I reckon that'll be
about as welcome as a pork chop in Jerusalem."

Act your age not your shoe size

Behaving immaturely

"Oh good onya, ya wanker,
why don't you act your age not your shoe size."

A face that only a mother could love

Fairly unattractive

"It's not his fault he's got
a face that only a mother could love."

A little more choke it would've started

To pass wind

"Careful Shauno,
a little more choke and that would've started."

All over it like a rash
on top of things

"Iv'e never seen Fred so keen,
he's all over it like a rash."

All piss and wind
Someone that is all talk and no action

"Are you still goin on about that ya stupid bastard."

"Don't listen to him mate, he's all piss and wind."

All the go these days
Something that is the latest craze

"Yeh fair dinkum, pole dancin,
I see lots of chicks doin it,
it's all the go these days."

A lot on his plate
He is very busy or taking on too much

"Tezzas a bit shirty don't ya think,"

"Na he's alright mate,
he's just got a bit on his plate at the moment."

All over the place like a drunkin spider
Highly intoxicated

"Mate I think Mary had one too many glasses of bubbly,
shez all over the place like a drunkin spider."

Always in the Shit

I am always in trouble

"Geez wadda ya done mate,
Jackie looks likes she's got the shit's with ya."

"That's nothin new,
I'm always in the shit,
it's only the depth that varies."

Australians being Aussies

Another nail in the coffin

An activity that will ensure my death

"That's the way Burty ava ciggy, and put another nail in your coffin."

Any slower he'd be dead

He is very very slow

"Bloody hell Fred, lift the pace mate, fair dinkum, if he moved any slower he'd be dead"

A Rooster one day, feather duster the next

Prime Minister to a clerical assistant

"Well I'll be buggered! Av a look at im now, A Rooster one day, feather duster the next."

Arse about face

The wrong way round

"That's not the way to do it ya drongo, you've got it arse about face."

Arse over tit
Falling over yourself head first

"Watch where ya goin or you'll go arse over tit."

As crooked as a dogs hind leg
This is not straight

"Ya call this straight,
it looks as crooked as a dog's hind leg."

A shit - Load
Huge Quantity

"It's alright for im,
he's got a shit-load of money."

As subtle as a kick in the guts
Fairly straight forward and to the point

"Good onya Joey, now she's crying.
You're about as subtle as a kick in the guts sometimes."

As thick as two planks of wood
Not real smart

"How would Jacko know?
He's thick as two planks of wood that bloke."

As ugly as a bulldog chewing a wasp

Now that's pretty ugly

"He's a cranky old bugger!
you should see im when he goes off,
he's as ugly as a bulldog chewing a wasp."

At the drop of a hat

To do something without hesitation

"Mate I wouldn't miss it for the world,
I'd be there at the drop of a hat."

Ava go ya mug

Have a descent attempt old chappy

"It's a game of cricket, ya suppose ta hit the ball,
ava go ya mug"

Away with the pixies

Day dreaming, in another world

"What was Fiona thinking?"

"I dunno Flo, she must have been
away with the pixies."

Awning over the toy shop

A mans beer belly covering the reproductive organs

"Now that's what I call a beer gut Thomo,"

"I paid a lot of money for this mate,
I call it me awning over the toy shop."

Back of Bourke
A long way out

"Bloody hell!
ya took ya time gettin here Jonno,
where ja go back of Bourke."

Back yourself
Have faith in oneself

"Get in there, ava go,
and just back yourself mate."

Barkin up the wrong tree
Following the incorrect lead

"Billy thought I might of been interested
in joining his political party,
he's barkin up the wrong tree there I can tell ya."

Bang like a dunny door in the wind

Frequent promiscuous activities

"Back in my day, some of the girls used to bang like a dunny door in the wind."

Beatin around the bush

Not getting straight to the point

"Bluey just say what you have to say, and stop beatin around the bush."

Belly flop

Diving in the pool belly first

"Did ya see Jacko dive in the pool? It was the biggest belly flop you'll ever see."

Berko

Quiet mad

"You should av seen her go berko, when Billy called her a sheila."

The most notable method of concealment was *cockney rhyming slang*. Rhyming slang created an idiom type sentence out of two or more words, the last of which rhymes with the intended word. For example, "plates of meat" were "feet" and "hit the frog and toad" was "hit the road."

Better hit the frog and toad *(Rhythmic)*   Hit the road

I'd better go home

"Well fella's that 'll do me,
I better hit the frog and toad."

Aside from rhyming slang, another method the convicts used to conceal their true meaning was to turn the meaning of a word upside down. For example, "**bastard**" or "**ratbag**" were used as terms of endearment as well as insults. The only way to know up from down was to infer from the tone of the sentence.

As is to be expected, the combination of novel words, rhyming slang and tonal communication had the authorities at a loss. This often allowed the convicts to make them the butt of ridicule. A good example of this can be found in the memoirs of

Captain James Rowntree:

On Monday of this week a Welsh convict named Jones called me "a Fair Dinkum Arsehole". For such insolence I was about to pistol whip him when Jones quickly started rambling. The funny thing was that it turns out that "Fair Dinkum" actually reverses the insult which follows. By calling me "a Fair Dinkum arsehole" he was saying that I am, in some way, the farthest thing possible away from an arsehole.

Feeling quite chuffed with myself I refrained from beating the man. I have decided to play along with their folly. In the last few days I have been called a "Fair dinkum Prick", Dick, Cows Tit and some really vulgar words that I would not put to paper. It has takentime but I have finally gained respect from these horrid convicts "

12 th February, 1839 *

Best thing since sliced bread

This is really really good

"You bet ya bottom dollar on that one Trev,
I reckon it's the best thing since sliced bread."

Just because the yanks invented the machine,
doesn't mean we can't use the saying,
it's a bloody ripper!!

Better half

Husband or wife

"Gidday Mick, ja bring the better half
to keep an eye on ya tonight."

Between you me and the gate post

Between you and myself and no-one else

"Between you, me and the gate post,
I think Joey's missus is leaving im."

Bewdy Mate   (Beauty mate)

Thank you my Good Fellow

"Righto Jonno Iv'e gotta kilo of snags
and a carton of piss, we're good to go."

"Bewdy mate,
you're a legend"

Big kahunas   Huge breast

"Whadja reckon Pete?"

"Yep I agree, they are some seriously big kahunas."

Big notes himself   Talk oneself up

"He's not as good as he thinks,
he just big notes himself."

Billy lids   (Rhythmic)   The Kids (children)

"Yeh mate, It's just me, the missus and the billy lids."

Bit off more than he could chew   He took on too much

"Poor old Robbo's in deep brown stuff,
he bit off more than he could chew this time."

Blind leadin the Blind

The unsure leading the unsurer

"Mate they haven't got a clue this lot,
it's like the blind leadin the blind."

Bludger

A person who will avoid work

"He hasn't worked a day in his life, he's just a bludger."

Bobs your uncle

And everything is OK

"Ya just put the whatsymacallit in there,
and the other thingo in here,
and there ya have it,
Bob's your uncle."

Brickies cleavage

An Australian workman bending over to reveal his bum crack

"Davo pull ya shorts up mate,
we don't wanna see your brickies cleavage."

Brown eye

Showing your bum hole

"It wasn't me mate, Jacko was in the back,
he's the one who chucked a brown eye at the coppers."

Brown noser

Someone who is very attentive around the boss

"I know why he's gettin the job mate,"

"Yeh it's cause he's got his nose so for up the bosses arse,
no wonder they call im a brown noser."

Buckleys Chance

You have no chance of that happening

"She thinks your a drop kick mate,
you've got buckleys chance of her goin out with you."

Buggalugs

An affectionate term for a mischievous person
or if you cannot remember their name

"Is Buggalugs comin along to the footy on the weekend?"

Bugger me dead

I am totally surprised

"Whadda ya mean, you haven't got time
Bugger me dead!
It only takes a few minutes."

Bugger that for a joke — I am not doing that

"I'm not goin up there, bugger that for a joke."

Built like a brick shithouse — Very well built human

"I wouldn't mess with im mate, he's built like a brick shithouse."

Bum nuts — Eggs

"Have ya got any free range bum nuts left mate?"

Bundy — Short for Bundaberg Rum

Bundaberg Rum Distillery located in mid to south east Queensland.

Bun in the oven   Pregnant

"Beryl do you think Marge is putting on weight,"

"Well she better have she's got a bun in the oven."

Bush telly   The night sky

"This is the life ..Hermie,
sittin round the camp fire,
couple of beers watchin the bush telly.
bloody beautiful!"

Busier than a one armed Sydney cab driver with the crabs   Over run with work

"Howz the preparations for ya sisters
weddin comin along Billy?"

"Oh mate I'm busier than a one armed
Sydney cab driver with crabs."

Busier than a blue arse fly   Extremely busy

"I'll hafta cancel this arvo,
I'm busier than a blue arsed fly."

Busier than a centipede doin up his shoe laces

Now that is busy

"Macka can't make it tonight fella's,
he reckons he's
busier than a centipede doin up his shoe laces."

Bush telegraph   Tell someone something that gets passed on very quickly

"We don't need any of that mod con stuff.
Once Beryl and Margo start yappin,
the news will get out there fairly quick,
those pair are like the bush telegraph round here."

Bush Week

Said by someone who thinks they are being made part of a scam

"How much doe's it cost to get in?"
"Im' not payin that,
wadda they think this is bush week!"

Butter wouldn't melt in your mouth

Someone may appear to be prim and proper person

"Cheryl's a nice enough sort of lady isn't she,"

"Yeh, yad think butter wouldn't melt in her mouth."

---

slang
\slang\, n. [cf. sling.] a fetter worn

fetter \FET-uhr\, noun:
1. A chain or shackle for the feet; a bond; a shackle.
2. Anything that confines or restrains; a re-

idiom n. A speech form or an expression of a given language that is peculiar to itself grammatically or cannot be understood from the individual

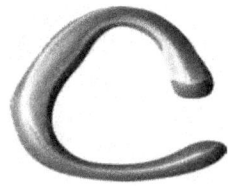

Call a spade a spade
speaks their mind

"There's no flies on Shazza,"

"Your not wrong there, she certainly calls a spade a spade."

Call it stumps
Time to finish what you are doing

"Come on Deano, it's time to go home mate.
lets call it stumps for the night."

Camp as a row of tents
Homo-sexual's

"Yeh but mate, they're as camp as a row of tents."

"Bloody hell Robbo they're not from outer space,
come on lets go, or we'll miss the first bit of the show."

Can't take it with you
When you die your money stays

"Me and Cheryl are thinkin about takin off,
and becomin grey nomads for a couple of years."

"Ya may as well Brucey ya can't take it with ya."

Carked it
It is dead

"Mate howz that old Holden of yours goin?"

"Na she's finally carked it."

Carryin on like a pork chop
Getting really upset

"You should've seen im go off,
he was carryin on like a pork chop"

Catcha later
Will see you at a later time

"Mate I've gotta hit the frog and toad,
so I'll catcha later."

Cats out of the bag
The secret is known

"We tried to keep it under wraps,
but now the cats out of the bag."

Caught with his pants down
An embarrassing situation

"He thought he was pretty good,
but he took it too far and ended up
gettin caught with his pants down,
didn't he."

Char some mystery bags — Cook sausages on the barbeque
(it's a mystery cause ya dunno what's in em)

"Come round for a feed later Jacko?
We're gunna char some mystery bags on the barby."

Cheesed off — Angry at something

"Whadja goin do that for ya knob head,
now shez really cheesed off."

Chewed the fat — Having a chat

"We sat round for a while, had a beer, and chewed the fat."

Chinnwag — Conversation

"Fiona came round yestee,
we had a good old chinwag."

Chocka block — Full, filled up

"Bazz ya not gunna fit anything else in there.
she's chocka block."

Chockers — Very full

"Cant fit another thing in,
she's absolutely chockers."

Chook raffle (Meat raffle)

An Aussie tradition of raising money
for surf club, footy team ect, by
selling tickets to win a
Chicken, meat or seafood tray, normally
held Friday afternoons at the local pub

Chucka Leftie — Turn left up here James

"Hey I think we just missed the turn off.
No worries,
just chucka leftie up here, and we'll be right."

Chuck a vee — Make a u turn

"Oh shit! we forgot to pack the bait."

"No Wukkin furries,
I'll just chuck a vee up here,
and we'll go back and get it."

Chuck a wobbly — Throw a tantrum

"There's no need to chuck a wobbly,
just cause ya couldn't get tickets for the game."

Cock and Bull story — Not an entirely true story

"Whadda load of rubbish!
That's nothin more than a cock and bull story."

Copped an earfull

Someone is very upset and letting you know about it.. Very loudly

"Mate you should've heard Jacko's missus go off last night, he copped an earfull when he got home."

Cop it on the chin

Take it as it comes

"Jonno won't care, he's the sought of bloke that'll cop it on the chin."

Couldn't catch a cold

Rarely catches a fish

"Took Kev fishin in the tinnie last week, fair dinkum mate, he couldn't catch a cold."

Couldn't fight his way out of a wet paper bag

Weak

"Bazza's weak as piss mate, he couldn't fight his way out of a wet paper bag."

Couldn't organise a root in a brothel

Organisation skills rated at 0

"Mate he's bloody useless,
he couldn't organise a root in a brothel."

Cow cockey

An Australian dairy farmer

"He won't make it in the big smoke,
he's a ridgy didge cow cocky."

Crack onto

Trying to pick someone up

"Have a look at Bluey trying to crack onto
that sheila at the bar...... he's got no hope."

Crickey (1838)

Total Surprise

"Crickey, ya bloody woofed that down,
ya must of been hungry Trev."

Crook as a dog

Not well at all

"Won't be able to make it in today Rexy,
I'm as crook as a dog."

Crook in the guts

Feeling sick in the stomach

"Joey ya still right to come fishin tomorrow?"

"Na mate, I'm still crook in the guts,
from those oysters I ate yesterdee"

"He's so mean he wouldn't even let his dog drink from a mirage"

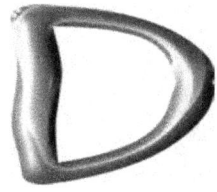

Dad n Dave
(Rhythmic)   Shave

"Better ava Dad n Dave, before we go out don't cha reckon."

Dead as a doornail
Not working - dead

"The engine's shot mate, she's dead as a doornail."

Dead marine
Empty beer bottle

"Must be your shout Harry, Iv'e got a dead marine over here."

Deadly treadly
Push bike

"Hey Wrighty, check out me new deadly treadly."

Dead set
I believe this to be correct

"Jen said she'd definitely turn up this time, dead set."

Deaf as a post
Unable to hear

"Ya can talk till the cows come home.
He won't hear ya,
he's deaf as a post."

Different kettle of fish
It is not the same

"Oh you want me to take holidays,
I thought ya said somethin else
now that's a different kettle of fish."

Didn't even touch the sides
Went down very quickly

"Oh that's better,
I was so bloody thirsty,
it didn't even touch the sides."

Doesn't know shit from clay
Not real bright

"Jonno reckons we should go ahead with it."

"Mate Im tellin ya,
he doesn't know shit from clay."

Doesn't measure up   Is not up to a certain standard

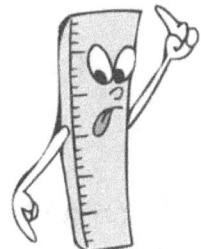

"We hafta let im go.
He just doesn't measure up
to the other players."

Dog and Bone   (Rhythmic)   Telephone

"Yeh I'll give im a call on the old dog and bone."

Dogs breakfast   Messy

"Ya should've seen the mess he made,
it looks like a dogs breakfast."

Don't be a stranger   Do not leave it too long
before we next meet

"Righto then Margo, don't be a stranger,
we'll catch ya later."

Dogs eye   (rhythmic}   A meat pie

"Wadda ya want Jacko."

"Think I'll go the old dogs eye with a bit of
dead horse, thanks mate."

Don't fret your freckle

There is no need for concern

"Righto Jackie, there's no need to fret your freckle.
I'll get to you in a minute."

Don't come the raw prawn

Please do not take me for a fool

"Are ya tellin me you knew about this.
Don't come the raw prawn with me mate."

Don't piss on me back and tell me that it's rainin

Transparent or misleading

"So ya reckon you went home before the pub shut,
we saw you leave with the barmaid,
so don't piss on me back and tell me that it's rainin."

Don't work to hard　　　　　　Do not over do it

"Righto Bazza, I've gotta fly mate,
don't work too hard."

Down the gurgler　　　　　　Lost what you had

"We lost it all mate,
down the gurgler."

Dragin ya feet　　　　　　Being real slow

"Keep up son, and stop dragin ya feet."

Drivin the porcelain bus　　　　Throwing up in the toilet

"I was feelin pretty crook when I got home,
I ended up drivin the porcelain bus,
most of the night."

Dry as a dead dingo's donga　　　Extremely dehydrated

"A schooner thanks luv.
I'm as dry as a dead dingo's donga."

Dunno　　　　　　　　　　I am not sure

"What about you brownie,
you right for this Fridee night?"

"Dunno yet, give us a sec and I'll have a look."

Dunnarunna

Has taken off

"Mate I haven't got a clue where he is, he's dunnarunna."

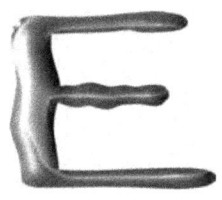

Eggin im on

To cheer on

"He'll be fine, we just need to egg im on a bit."

Even blind Freddy could see that

It is so plainly obvious

"That pass was a mile forward, even blind Freddy could see that."

Everything but the kitchen sink

Carrying or packing everything

"We're all packed and ready to go,
Margo's takin everything but the kitchen sink."

Every man and his dog

Everyone is coming, even their dogs

"Mate it's gunna be great, I can't wait.
They reckon every man and his dog will be there."

Edna like a horse

Not very attractive

"Your jokin aren't ya,
from where I'm sittin,
she's got a edna like a horse."

Fair dinkum   A true fact

"I saw it meself mate,
fair dinkum,
it was about an 18 metre croc."

Fair enough   Ok that's fair

"Yeh I agree with ya on that one, fair enough mate."

Fair crack of the whip   Fair and equal opportunity

"Fair crack of the whip Jonesy,
let Simmo's have his say will ya."

Fair go mate   Give me a break

"Are you gunna make me queue up again,
oh fair go mate."

Fart arse around   Playing around, having fun

"Jacko's not fair dinkum about this,
he just wants to fart arse around."

Fat chance   No hope at all

"Tezza say's he's gunna share his winnings,
there's a fat chance of that happenin don't cha reckon."

Feelin a bit peckish   Feeling hungry

"Whadda ya reckon we grab a feed
at the pub, I'm feelin a bit peckish."

Fell on deaf ears   They did not hear what I had to say

"I tried to tell the dope it wouldn't work,
but it fell on deaf ears."

Fell out of the ugly tree   Not very desirable

"Have ya had a look in the mirror lately Dicko,
ya look like ya just fell out of the ugly tree."

Fightin like cats and dogs   Arguing amongst themselves

"Joaney doesn't agree with Bill,
so their at it again, fightin like cats and dogs."

Find out nosey

I cannot reveal

"Where have you been for the last half hour Macka."

"Find out nosey."

Fit as a Malley Bull

Strong and fit

"Howsha been Mick?"

"Me ...couldn't be better.
I'm as fit as a Malley bull"

Flat out like a lizard drinkin

Really busy

"Hughsey ya comin round for a barby?"

"Not today Tunksey. I haven't got time mate.
I'm flat out like a lizard drinkin."

Flog it off

To sell something really cheap

"It's buggered mate, so I'm just gunna hafta to flog it off."

Forkin out big bickkies

Paying out a lot of money

"He's spendin heaps on his car."

"I know mate, he's been forkin out big bikkies."

Freeze your tits off

Extremely cold

"How cold is it down in Tassie, at the moment Hermie?"

"Cold enough to freeze your tits off."

From Go to Woe

Start to finish

"I stuck with it all the way, yep from Go to Woe"

Full as a goog

I have had enough to eat

"Wanna nuther snag mate?"

"Couldn't eat another thing, thanks Pete.
I'm full as a goog."

Full as a butchers dog

I am lucky to be fed well

"Thanks Ma, now that was a feed.
I'm as full as a butchers dog."

Full of it

Over confident, Arrogant

"Jonesy reckons he got third division in lotto."

"Ya don't believe that shit do ya,
Jonsey's full of it."

Funny as a fart in an elevator

Not even a bit funny

"Good one Smiddy, that's about as
funny as a fart in an elevator."

Funny farm

Mental Institution

"If Joey keeps this up, we'll have to send
him off to the funny farm."

Ganda
To have a look

"Ava gander at that, will ya."

Get that indya
Get that into you- please help yourself

"There ya go mate,
me own version of spaghetti bog, get that indya."

Get your arse into gear
Speed this process up

"Come on Breno, stop muckin round,
and get your arse into gear."

Get the giddy up
Hurry up

"Come on Stevo, where gunna miss Gilly bat.
Get the giddy up."

Gidday ya old bastard
Hello old fellow

"Gidday ya old bastard.
Wadda ya been up too."

Give it a Burl
Try it out

"Ya should giver a go Kev."

"Yeh righto then, I'll give it a burl."

Give im a bit of curry
To direct abuse at someone

"I wasn't happy about what he had to say,
so I give im a bit of curry about it."

Give it the flick
To toss away

"What happened to your new watch Pete?"

"It was bloody useless,
so I gave it the flick."

Give it the once over
Quickly examine something

"Yeh bring it round Robbo, and I'll give it the once over mate."

Go root a boot
Please keep your opinion to yourself

"I don't care whatcha think,
you can all go root a boot as far as I'm concerned"

Goin like hot cakes

They are selling really fast

"Ya betta get in quick Flo,
cause they're goin like hot cakes."

Goin thru me like a dose of salts

Go through something quickly

"That chilli I had was so bloody hot!
It's goin thru me like a dose of salts."

Goin drain the one eyed trouser snake

Man having a wee

"I'll be back in a tic,
Iv'e gotta goin drain the one eyed trouser snake."

Goes off like Chinese New Year

Something fun packed

"Mate were gunna hava a ball at the Country music festival,
she goes off like Chinese new year."

Goin at it like rabbits

Frantic sexual encounter

"I went round to Stevo's place yesterdee,
and the front door was open,
so I walk in.. and bugger me dead!!
Him and his missus were goin at it like rabbits."

Good night Nurse

It's all over

"Mate he drank 15 schooners at the pub. then when he got home he started on the sambucca, and well, it was all over. Good night nurse."

Got his head so far up his arse

Will not take your advice or is just plain arrogant

"I tried to tell im, but he's got his head so far up his arse, he just doesn't listen."

Got the rough end of the pineapple

Unlucky in that situation

"Mate ya wouldn't believe it, but Mick had ta stay back again. He won't be able to make it."

"Geez he got the rough end of the pineapple, didn't he."

Gotcha by the short and curlies

I have you check mate on that situation

"I betcha didn't know that didja Einstein?
I gotcha by the short and curlies on that one."

Gotta a few roos loose in the paddock

Not real bright

"He's a nice enough sort of bloke,
but I think he's got a few roos loose in the paddock."

Great Australian salute

Chasing away flies from your face

"We hadda bloody good weekend.
except for those dam flies.
we were all giving each other the Great Australian Salute."

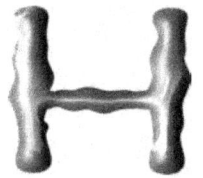

Hair of the dog

A concoction drink intended to cure a hangover

"Howja pull up this mornin Thomo?"

"Oh mate, I'm a bit crook.
I think I need a hair of the dog."

Handles like a dog on lino

Lino is a slippery floor covering,
you get the picture

"Mate I took it for a spin, and to tell ya the truth,
she handles like a dog on lino."

Hangin for a piss

I really have to go and urinate

"Hold onto that thought Davo, I'll be back in a tick.
I'm hangin for a piss."

Happy as a worm comin home from a fishin trip

Happy as a Bastard on Fathers Day

Not really all that delighted

"I worked all these years and got bugger all.
I felt about as
happy as a bastard on fathers day."

Happy as a worm coming home from a fishin trip

About as happy as can be

"Kev's rapt with the result.
He's about as happy as a
worm coming home from a fishin trip."

Happy little vegemite

Someone is joyful

"There's no doubt about it,
but young Jayda's a happy little vegemite,
isn't she."

Happy as Larry

To be content and happy

"How are you Shauno?"

"Mate I'm doin well.
Happy as Larry."

WHO'S LARRY.

The Australian boxer Larry Foley (1847 - 1917)
Foley was a successful boxer, who never lost a fight
He retired at 32 and collected a purse of 1000 pound for
his last fight.
We can expect that he was known to be happy
with his lot in the 1870's, just when the phrase is first cited

Hard pill to swallow

I don't really want to believe it, although I will have to

"Did ya hear Jonno own up to Macka,
that the best team won on the day."

"That would av been a hard pill for him to swallow."

Hava good one

Hope you have a good day

"Righto mate I'm off, so I'll catch ya later."

"Yeh, hava good one."

havin a Captain Cook

Have to take a snakes hiss (Rhythmic) Piss

I must go to the lavatory to relieve myself

"Hold my seat for me will ya,
I have to take a snakes hiss."

Havin a Captain Cook (Rhythmic) Look

I will go and have a look

"Where's Jonno gone?"
"Dunno mate,
I'll go and have a captain cook."

Havin a perve Checking out a rather attractive human specimen

"Come on Billy it's your shout."

"Hang on mate, I'm havin a perve."

He ran like a hairy goat Ran rough and slow

"Your's ran like a hairy goat!"
"You can't talk mate, your horse is still running."

Headlights on high beam When the nipples are erect

"It must be cold out,
Shazza's got er headlights on high beam."

He's a bit tinny
Lucky

"Has Bazza won again?"

"Yep, that boy's a bit tinnie."

He's got a bit of mongrel in him
Has quite an aggressive nature

"Wadda bout MG, now he can play footy."

"Yeh he's got a bit of mongrel in im that's needed."

He's got more corrugation than a water tank
Ripples in his beer belly

"Ava look at the gut on big Kev,
he's got more corrugation than a water tank."

He's havin a Barry Crocker
(Rhythmic) Shocker

He is not going very well

"Joey's dropped the ball again,
he's havin a Barry Crocker."

(Barry Crocker is an iconic singer in Australia)

He's in more shit than Ned Kelly

He is in deep trouble

(an Australian bushranger)

"Dunno how Bretto's gunna get outta this one, he's in more shit than Ned Kelly."

He's so big he has his own postcode

He is a huge man

" Franky's a big boy isn't he?"

"Mate he's so big he has his own postcode."

He's so thin he'd have to run round in the shower to get wet

A very thin male

"Geez Bazza's lost some frigin weight? He's so thin he'd have to run round the shower to get wet."

He's shootin blanks

He has had a vasectomy, or is unable to father a child naturally

"I don't think she know's who the father is."

"Well it can't be Jonno's, he's shootin blanks."

He thinks his shit doesn't stink

Someone thinks they're fairly special

"Jonno picked up all the awards, at last nights ceremony."

"Yeh I know,
now he thinks his shit doesn't stink."

Hit in the bread basket

Hit in the stomach

"Mal was the best at passin the footy,
every time, it would hit ya in the breadbasket."

Hit in the jatz crackers

(Rhythmic)   Knackers

Hit in the testicles

"I tell ya, there's nothin worse
than being hit in the jatz crackers."

Hit the ground running

Going at a rapid pace

"Yeh Shazza started Tuesdee, got straight into it too,
she hit the ground running."

Hold your horses

Do not be in such a rush

"Righto hold your horses, I'll be there in a jiffy."

Holy snappin duck shit

Gosh I am totally surprised

"Holy snappin duck shit!
He finally won one."

Hope all his chickens turn into emus and kick down his dunny door

Wishing bad luck on someone

"No fairs fair... No hard feelin's.
I just hope all his chickens
turn into emus and kick his dunny door down."

Hot under the collar

Someone is angry about something

"Yeh settle down mate, it's only a game.
Ya gettin a bit hot under the collar."

How long is a piece of string

No one knows the answer

"Do you think Beryl will like this?"

"Who know's mate,
that's like askin how long is a piece of string"

How ya goin . good

How are you . good

(Sometimes we will ask you a question, and answer it for you.)

"Burt ya old bastard. how ya goin, Good?"

Howsha weekend

How was your weekend

"Morning Mary, howsha weekend?"

I couldn't give a rats arse

I couldn't give a rats arse   I'm not particularly interested

"Flo thinks the boys are still at the pub."

"I couldn't give a rats arse, where they are.
I'm watchin a farmer wants a wife."

I need that like a submarine needs a screen door

                  Just had more bad luck delivered to him

"Ya gotta be kiddin me!
This happened yesterdee as well.
I needed that like a submarine needs a screen door."

I'd like to be a fly on the wall

                                          I would love to hear or see that

"Davo's missus is going to hit the roof, when he gets home. I'd like to be a fly on the wall, to hear her go off."

If I want any shit I'll squeeze ya head

                                      If I require your opinion I shall ask for it

"Thanks for that dickhead! But if I want any shit I'll squeeze ya head."

If I've told you once I've told you a thousand times

                                            I have told you over and over

"If I've told you once I've told you a thousand times. ya tilt the glass when ya pourin a beer."

If it was rainin palaces I would get hit with the dunny door

                                          I am not at all lucky

"You'll be right Alfi, what could possibly go wrong?"

"I'm tellin ya knowin my luck, if it was rainin palaces I would get hit with the dunny door."

I'll have ya guts for garters

I'm very upset with you

"Im not in the mood for ya shit Jacko, so pull ya head in, or I'll have ya guts for garters."

I'm absolutely buggered

I am very exhausted

"Come on Billy, just one more game,"
"No way mate, I'm absolutely buggered"

I'm all ears

I will listen intently

"Did ya hear me?
"Yeh sorry, go on mate, I'm all ears."

I'm as dry as a pommies bathmat

Sometimes it's too cold in the motherland to get wet

"Mate it must be beer o'clock,
I'm as dry as a Pommies bathmat."

I'm buggered, Broke, and bewildered.

(stuffed, under paid, and over worked.)

I'm Cactus

I am not in a good place right now

"You don't understand, if you can't fix it,
I'm cactus."

I'm off, like bucket of prawns in the sun

I shall see you later

"It's time to go Wally, I'm off,
like a bucket of prawns in the sun."

I'm so hungry I could eat a horse and chase the jockey

Now that is one hungry chap

"Howzit goin Smiddy, you up for a feed big fella?"

Bloody oath mate, I'm so hungry I could eat a horse, and chase the jockey."

In two shakes of a lambs tail

It will happen very quickly

"I'll be with you in two shakes of a lambs tail."

Is the Pope catholic

This fact is true

"Bloody Oath I'll have a beer, is the pope catholic?"

It will take you a month of Sundays

A long period of time

"It will take you a month of Sundays to finish that."

It doesn't get any better than this
Life is pretty good

"Have a look at us, kickin back on your boat,
a cold stubbie, prawns,
it doesn't get any better than this."

It'll all come out in the wash
It will all work out

"You don't hafta worry about that mate,
it'll come out in the wash."

It's a cracker
That is very good

"I love what you've done with the VeeDub Robbo."

"Thanks Graham,
It's a cracker isn't it."

It's a goer
It will happen

"It's stopped rainin, so yep,
the games on mate, it's a goer."

It's a rip snorter
It's something special

"I'm gunna take me new fishin rod,
it's a rip snorta!"

It's a bloody ripper
It is fantastic

"Just got myself a new barby,
4 burner, with one of those rotisseries,
it's a bloody ripper!"

It's Cactus
It is not working

"I've got no hope of fixing that heap mate,
it's cactus."

It's so cold it would freeze the balls off a brass monkey
Very very cold

"Howz the weather your way mate?"

"Bazza it's so cold,
it would freeze the balls off a brass monkey."

I've had a gut full
Have had enough of your behaviour

"Come on mate, Iv'e had a gut full of ya shit.
now what really went on."

I've had it since Adam was a boy
It is very old

"Simmo. what's that contraption in ya shed."

"That old thing.
I've had it since Adam was a boy."

I've seen better legs on a pool table

                                        Those legs are not that desirable

"Burt reckon's his missus has got great legs,"
"Ya jokin aren't ya,
mate I've seen better legs on a pool table."

"If I had a dog that looked like you, I'd shave it's arse and make it walk backwards."

Jack of that   I have had enough

"Howza new job goin Stewie?"

"They wanted me to stay back again,
so I got Jack of that, and told im to shove it."

Jack and Jill   (Rhythmic)   The bill

"Now that was a bloody good feed,
I'll just grab the Jack and Jill, and we'll head off."

Joe Blow   An average fellow

"Yeh righto hero,
so ya only fixed a leakin tap,
any old Joe Blow could do that."

Just quietly   It is only my opinion

"I think Flemo will bowl alright
over in England this time, just quietly."

Joker

Someone you do not respect

"That joker, Iv'e never liked him."

Jumpin round like a flea on a dog

Unsettled

"Righto then Bazza, make up your mind mate,
ya jumpin round like a flea on a dog."

Just round the corner

Not far, and yet further than you think

"When Fred says it's just round the corner,
you'd better take a cut lunch.
It could be 100 Klicks away."

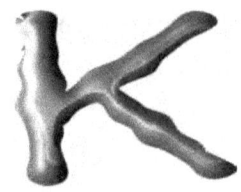

Kaffufle — Disturbance

"It wasn't that bad,
I don't know what all the kaffufle was about."

Kangaroo Court — Outside the bounds of the judicial process

"That isn't right mate, what is this a Kangaroo court."

Keen as mustard — Wanting to do something with full enthusiasm

"Mate he'll do it for sure,
he's as keen as mustard."

Keep an ear out — Listen out for a sign

"Good on ya Fred,
keep an ear out would ya,
they might come back."

Kern an Oath mate

That is definitely right

"You reckon ya gunna catch a fish with that rod."

"Kern oath mate,
she's me old favourite"

Knackered

Extremely tiered

"Wadda ya been up to Jonno, ya look buggered?"

"Iv'e been helpin Bluey move house,
I'm feelin pretty knackered."

Knee high to a grasshopper

Really small

"Iv'e known Joey since he was knee high to a grasshopper."

Knickers in a knot   Becoming irritated

"Yeh righto mate.. don't get ya knickers in a knot.
I was only havin a go at ya."

Knob head   Dick head   Richard Cranium

"Did ya hear what Jacko had to say last night
about the Tigers,"

"He's clueless mate, bloody knob head."

Lady muck

A very well to do lady

"Ava look at Katie would ya,
she's been waited on hand and foot.
Anyone would think she's Lady muck."

Lights on but no ones home

Someone that lacks intelligence

"Mate he tries, but he just doesn't get it."

"Yeh I think the lights on but no one's home."

Lemon

A dud, does not work

"I'd hate to tell ya Jimmy,
but it looks like ya bought a lemon."

Like putting Dracula in charge of the blood bank

He is not the man for the job

"Ya can't put Smiddy in charge of the beer fridge.
That's like putting Dracula in charge of the blood bank."

Lippie (he's a bit)

He speaks without thinking

"Jonno worked alright today Bazza."

"Yeh he's a bit lippie, but he's alright."

Lollie water

Soft drink-Soda

"Whadda ya drinkin lollie water for Kev, that stuff will rot ya guts."

Looks like somethin the cat dragged in

This is a total mess

"Wadda reckon Matty?"

"Mate it looks like somethin the cat dragged in."

Lower than a snakes belly

Someone not to be trusted

"I wouldn't buy anything off Willy, he's lower than a snakes belly that bloke."

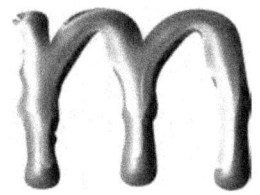

Mad as a cut snake — A little bit insane

"Ja see Tezza go off at the footy yesterdee?
He's as mad as a cut snake, the silly bastard."

Make tracks — I had better be on my way

"Anyway Whitie, I'd better make tracks,
gotta pick up the Billy lids from school."

Man's not a camel — I need a drink immediately

"Come on ya doppy bastard, finish it up.
it's your shout..
A man's not a camel you know."

Man's not a Camel

Map of Tassie

Hair line shape of a women's bikini line

(A state of Australia)

"So Billy's leans out the window,
as we're drivin past, and yells out,
show us ya map of Tassie."

"Yeh he can be a wanker at times."

Misery guts

Someone who complains constantly

"Geez you've turned into a misery guts lately.
all we hear is ya wingin and whinin about bloody nothin."

More front than Myers

Bold and courageous

(A Department store with large window front)

" Bluey just walked straight up to them,
and tried to crack onto the blond piece."

"Yeh he's got more front than Myers that bloke."

More arse than class

Someone that is very lucky

"Robbo's got more arse than class,
he's picked three winners in a row."

Muckin around　　　　　　　　　　Playing around

"Righto ya bloody clowns,,
stop muckin around.
and we'll have this knocked off in no time."

Mystery bags　　　　　　　　　　Sausages

"Why do they call them mystery bags dad?"

"Cause mate,
you never know what's really in them."

A Friend's Prayer

"May the fleas of a thousand camels

infest the crotch

of the person who screws up your day,

and may their arms

be too short to scratch."

Amen

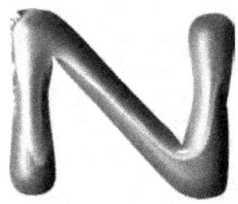

Nervous as a long tailed cat in a room full of rockin chairs

"Joey's shit scared mate!"

"I don't blame im..
I'd be as nervous as a long tailed cat in
a room full of rockin chairs. if I had to do that."

No flies on him   Confident without arrogance

"There's no way, I'd be game enough to do that."

"Yeh ya gotta hand it to Hughes'y, there's no flies on him."

No worries mate   I do not have any problems with that

"I can fix that, for ya Bazza,
no worries mate."

No Wukkin Furries   Not a problem   (no fuckin worries)

"Will you be there tomorrow mate."

"No wukkin furries,
I'll be there with bells on."

Not a pubic hair in it

Now that is very very close

"It's bloody close mate, not a pubic hair in it."

Not backwards in coming forward

Speaks their mind, free to offer an opinion

"Did you hear what Jan had to say?"

"Yeh, she's not backward in coming forward is she?"

Not the full quid

Is of lesser intelligence

"Tell me ya not takin Jonno with ya, he's not the full quid is he."

Not within cooee of here

It is far away

"Where the hell is Burke and Wills camp."

"Never heard of it luv,
it's not within cooee of here."

On a good wicket

Everything is going very well at present

"Looks as though Donny's got a new company car."

"Lets face it he's on a good wicket these days."

On the nose

Unpleasant odour

"How long av those prawns been out for,
they smell a bit on the nose."

One for Justin

Just in case

"Mate I've gotta take off,
I'll catch ya later,
I better take one of these sangers, for Justin."

One for Ron

Later on

"Ya headin off Tunks'y?"

"Yeh mate."

"Here take this stubbie with ya,
one for Ron."

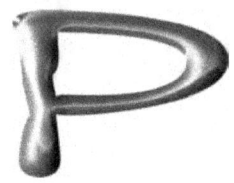

Packs a punch   Spicy strong tasting

"Bloody hell mate, that's packs a punch, what's in it."

Pass the dead horse   *{Rhythmic}* Tomato sauce

"Pass the dead horse will ya son."

Pat Malone   *{Rhythmic}* All Alone

"Who's there with ya Bluey?"

"No one mate, just here on me Pat Malone."

Piece of piss   Something requiring not much effort

"I'll take care of that for ya Gazza,
piece of piss,
I'll have it done in no time at all."

Pigs bum   No way

"They said your gunna take them up on their offer."
"Pigs bum...
I wouldn't touch it with a forty foot barge pole."

Piss head

Consumes a lot of the liquid amber fluid

"Davo's always at the pub.
He's just a bloody piss head isn't he."

Piss poor

That is very poor

"Ya should've at least shook his hand,
that's pretty piss poor mate."

Pissed as a cricket

Very drunk

"What about Jonesy last night."

"Yeh he had a few."

"A few, mate he was pissed as a cricket."

Pissed it all up against the wall

Spend a lot of your money on alcohol

"He's been here all day, and I reckon he's
pissed it all up against the wall."

Pocket Billiards

Adjusting your genitals

"What are ya doin there mate,
havin a game of pocket billiards."

"No mate just straighten'n up the boys."

Popular as a mangy dog

Unwanted and definitely not popular

"Jacko forgot to bring the grog..."

"Ya jokin, that would've made him
about as popular as a mangy dog."

Preggers

Pregnant

"I'm gunna be a dad, Donna's just found out she's preggers."

Pull the wool over my eyes

One is trying to deceive you

"Are you serious, or are you just trying to
pull the wool over my eyes."

Pull your head in

Hold your opinion to yourself

"It's not up to you dick head,
so best pull your head in."

Pussyfootin around

Tip toe in around

"Get in, get the job done,
and stop pussyfootin around you blokes."

Put all your eggs in one basket

Putting all your efforts into one thing only

"That's not a bad idea mate.
Ya just gotta be careful,
not to put all your eggs in one basket."

Pushin shit up hill

A task that is highly difficult

"It's gettin late,
you'll be pushin shit up hill,
to get that done before dark, I can tell ya."

Pushin Shit up hill

Australians being Aussies

Put the hard word on   Ask someone for sex

"Whad she slap ya for mate?
Ja put the hard word on her."

Puts hairs on your chest   Will make a man of you

"Eat it all up, and it'll put hairs on your chest."

Queensland   A State of Australia

There's only three states worth being in.
Queensland,
pissed,
or pissed in Queensland.

Quick smart   Be really quick

"Happy hour's nearly over Breno,
so ya better get here quick smart."

Rainin cats and dogs — Rain coming down hard

"Not literally raining cats and dogs, it's just bloody pourin down."

Rapt — Elated or delighted

"There were 26 applicants and I got the job, I'm rapt."

Reg Grundies (Rhythmic) — Undies - Underwear

"Enjoy your trip away Stevo, and don't forget to pack ya Reg Grundies."

Rip snorter — This is great

"How was the footy Billy?"

"Mate it was a rip snorter of a game, the Bulldogs scored right on full time to win."

Roo juice

Kangaroo petrol, not literally when your car is jumpy

"Mate, she drives like she's got a bit of roo juice in er."

Ropable

Gone past angry

"He'll be ropable, when he gets back and see's this mess."

Rough as guts

Course, disorderly and rude

"Jonno's sister come round yesterdee, geez... she can be as rough as guts at times, don't ya reckon."

Run rings around him

Beaten comprehensively

"Ponting's a much better player, he runs rings around that other bloke."

Proud to be an Aussie

Some of the things we did first

ESKY

In 1952 some blokes in the Malley company made a portable drink cooler, made of a steel box within a steel box, they put ice in between

...Plastic arrived in the 70's

We love these blokes

FREESTYLE (Australian Crawl)

Syd and Charles Cavill showed the world in 1902, and it become the standard in international competitions.

and check out these two little beauty's

Fanny Durack (left) and Mina Wylie

were the first two women to represent Australia in swimming at the Olympics.

They were club-mates in Sydney and completed an Australian quinella in the 100 m freestyle.

CALL GIRLS

Melbourne 1981, Brothel owners opened the first system for ordering prostitutes by phone

Good on us

HILLS HOIST

In 1946, good old Lance Hill welded some pipes together in his shed in Adelaide. He sold millions, and become the symbol in Aussie backyards

Remember as kids you used to swing on them.

KIWI BOOT POLISH

In 1906, William Ramsey and Hamilton McKellan of Melbourne had a shoe cream able to restore colour to faded leather .By 1920, they had sold 30 million tins

"Alright I know what ya thinkin,
why the hell is it called Kiwi Boot Polish,
well, Bill's missus was a New Zealander."
"We know who wears the pants
in that relationship don't we."

GRANNY SMITH APPLES

In 1868, Maria Smith grew a long lasting apple in her garden in Sydney, The kids then marketed it to the world

Thanks Granny

NOTEPAD

1902 a stationer from Launceston, Tasmania, J.A Birchall Produced bundles of paper with the sheets gummed together along the top

Those Tasweigens are an industrious lot.

THE PACEMAKER

Started in 1902, Sydney Women's Hospital developed a machine to keep a baby's heart beating.

In the 1970's, an Aussie Company developed a version that could last 20 years.

I'd reckon I'd get it checked around the 19 th year..................wouldn't you?

Say it don't spray it
Please speak without spitting

"Ok mate I get it,
but say it don't spray it."

Scarce as hens teeth
Something that is very uncommon

"I can't believe you got one,
they're as scarce as hens teeth."

See ya round like a rissole
Will see at a later time

"Gotta go mate, so I'll see ya round like a rissole"

Send er down Huey
Talkin to the man upstairs, send down the rain

"We need some rain,
sender down Huey."

She goes like the clappers

Travels at high speed

"She looks like a heap of shit Jonno."

"Don't you worry mate,
she goes like the clappers."

She's got a head on her like the south end of a north bound camel

Unpleasant to look at

"Mate, she's got a head on her like
the south end of a north bound camel."

Shit hit's the fan

There will be trouble

"Ya betta get home Bazza,
before the shit hit's the fan."

She'll be apples

Everything will be ok

"Ah don't worry bout it Mick,
there's always tomorrow,
she'll be apples."

Shoe string budget

Not much money to spend

"All your ideas are valid.
just remember, we are working on a
shoe string budget."

Shonky

Under handed, not totally honest

"Tell me you didn't buy that from the mob down the road,
they're as shonky as mate."

Shot imself in the foot

Made a mistake that will cause him grief

"I think he said too much,
and shot imself in the foot."

Show you the ropes

I will show you the way to do it

"It's easy Jacko, come along next week,
and I'll show you the ropes."

Sick as a dog

Not feeling well

"I won't be able to make it tonight Billy, I'm sick as a dog."

Sittin on the fence

Undecided- will not vote one way or the other

"Whoz gunna win the footy Smithy?"

"Dunno, I reckon both teams have a chance."

"Oh stop sittin on the fence mate and make a call."

Six of one and half a dozen of the other

It means the same thing

"Doesn't matter to me,
six of one half a dozen of another."

Just another smart arse

Smart arse

Someone who is clever or is sarcastic in a witty manner

"And Davo came back with one of his sarcastic remark's, he's such a smart arse some times."

So thin she wouldn't even cast a shadow

All skin and bone

"Shazza needs a good feed, she's so thin she wouldn't even cast a shadow."

Spat the dummy

Temper tantrum

"Where's Smiddy gone? He hasn't spat the dummy again, has he."

Stickin out like a stiffy in a pair of speedo's

(A pair of speedo's is a brief swimming costume)

It really stands out

"I didn't know you noticed."

"How could ya miss it ya doppy bastard, it's stickin out like a stiffy in a pair of speedo's."

Spittin chips

Very upset

How'd Davo take being dropped from the team?"

"Not good, he's spittin chips."

Sticks out like dogs balls

Very noticeable

"I can't go out with this big zit on my face, it sticks out like dogs balls."

Stiff Cheddar

Too Bad

"Jill has to realize that she can't have everything her own way, so stiff cheddar."

Stole my thunder   Took my applause

"Well I went to say something,
but Billy piped up, and stole me thunder didn't he."

Stone the bloody crows   Disbelief   very surprised

"Well stone the bloody crows!
So they say you're a star and on telly now."

Stones throw away   Not for away

"Where ya travellin to Timbuktu?
That's only a stones throw from here mate."

Stop ya wingin   Could you please cease that infernal whining

"You've been goin on about it all day,
will ya stop ya wingin."

Straight out of the horses mouth

Received information first hand

"Bloody oath it's fair dinkum!
I got it straight from the horses mouth."

Stunned mullet

In shock or disbelief

"I don't think he could believe it,
he just stood around like a stunned mullet."

Sweatin like a pregnant nun at confession

Very anxious

"Yep ya should've seen er, she was
sweatin like a pregnant nun at confession."

Take a chill pill
Relax   Breath   Do not stress

"Maz was so wound up,
I told her to relax and take a chill pill."

Take a cut lunch
It may be a long trip

"They live miles away from here,
ya need to take a cut lunch."

Take the bull by the horns
Take charge of a situation

"Look Robbo just take the bull by the horns and go for it."

Takin the Mickey out of
To tease - make fun of

"He got fired up mate.
But it was harmless enough,
Jonsey was just takin the Mickey out of im."

Talk under wet cement
Never stops talking

"Ya talkin about Janna?
Bloody hell mate, that girl can
talk under we cement."

Tickled pink
Happy and excited

"We let Flo know her scones were voted the best, she was tickled pink."

The town Bike
A woman who is known to be promiscuous

"When I knew her, she used to be known as the town bike."

The whole box and dice
Absolutely everything

"Mate she's got everything, the whole box and dice."

The coat hanger
The Sydney Harbour Bridge

The most fun you can have with your pants on

Having a great time

"Mate you should try it,
it's the most fun you can have with your pants on."

The pot callin the kettle black

Casting aspersions on others, when you are similar

"Your callin me a piss head!
now that's the pot callin the kettle black."

Thick as a brick

Not real bright

"Your jokin aren't ya?
Bluey's not capable of doin that.
He's thick as a brick."

Think outside the square

Think creatively without constraints

"Mate come on, get creative,
and think outside the square."

Threw a spanner in the works

Upset plans that are in motion

"That was goin great,
until Fred threw a spanner in the works."

Throws the toys out of the pram

Temper tantrum

"He always
throws the toys out of the pram,
when Ford gets up at Bathurst."

Thru to the keeper

To let something go

"Yeah I heard him,
but I just let it go thru to the keeper."

Tighter than a fishes bumhole

Finds it extremely hard to part with money

"Fred would jump the fence, to go to the drive in movies.
He's tighter than a fishes bumhole, I'm tellin ya."

To the naked eye Eyesight seeing something without binoculars

"To the naked eye, it looks further away."

"That's bloody obvious,
geez your a genius smithy."

Too bad so sad

That is such bad luck

"It' not my fault ya clumsy,
and fell over ya own feet.
Too bad so sad."

Tough titties

How unfortunate for you

"You lost the bet fair and square,
so tough titties big fella."

Trouble strife and the billy lids *(Rhythmic)* Wife and Kids

My wife and children

"Ya stayin for another Bluey?"

"Na boys that'll do me,
better get home to the trouble strife and the billy lids."

Tub er up I am going to have a bath/shower

"Yeh keep a seat warm for me will ya.
I'll be down shortly,
just gotta go and tub er up."

Two pot screamer One who cannot handle their liquor

"You should've seen Jenny last night,
talk about a two pot screamer,"

Tooin and froin undecided

" I dunno yet,
I keep tooin and froin.
I'll let ya know toomurra."

Ugly as a hat full of arseholes

Not the most attractive

"Mate have you had a geez in the mirror lately, you're about as ugly as a hat full of arseholes."

Up shit creek without a paddle

Not going extremely well

"Whydja go and tell im that for ya dickhead, now we're up shit creek without a paddle."

Use your loaf

(Rhythmic) head, bread, loaf

You need to think

"You know howda do it son, if you use your loaf, you'll figure it out."

Australians being Aussies

Up at sparrows fart

Awakens early in the morning with the birds

"Righto then I'm off to bed.
Got an early start tomorrow,
so I'll be up at sparrows fart."

Up and down like a yo yo

Going from one thought to another

"What happen to Jacko?
I thought he was comin out with us tonight."

"Dunno mate, at the moment he's up and down like a yo yo."

Verandah over the tool shed   Beer belly

"Geez Jacko's gotta gut on im hasn't he."

"Yeh, he reckon's it's his verandah over the tool shed."

Verbal diarrhoea   Talkin nonsense

"Geez you were speakin some verbal diarrhoea. last night Shauno."

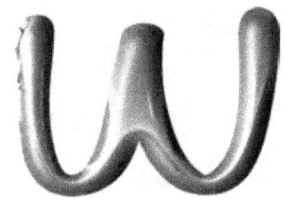

Wadda an absolute Spunk

What amazingly handsome fellow

"Beryl hava a geez at that bloke over there. Wadda absolute spunk!!"

Wadda load of codswollip

I find it hard to believe

"Billy reckons he didn't know."

"Coarse he bloody knew,
wadda load of codswollip."

Wadda ya know.

A way of starting a conversation,
what do you know

"Macka... How are ya mate? wadda ya know."

Wadda ya reckon

May I please have your opinion

"Davo have a look at this... I made it yesterdee.
Wadda ya reckon."

Waitin till the cows come home

You will be waiting a considerable while

"No I'll hafta do it meself,
if I wait for Harold,
I'll be waitin till the cows come home."

Wally Woofter

Rhythmic (Poofter)

"Went out with Bretto last night."

"Mate you know he's a Wally Woofter."

"What difference does that make ya dickhead.
I tell ya those blokes know how to party."

Wanker
A complete idiot

"Whadja do that for ya bloody wanker"

Was ya father a glass maker
I cannot see through you

"Was ya father a glass maker Stevo."

"No mate..."
"Then move out of the way, so I can see the telly"

Weak as piss
No internal fortitude

"Ya didn't need to say that behind his back, that's as weak as piss mate."

Wedding tackle
Testicles, balls, knackers, crowned jewels, jatz crackers, cods, go nads

"Yeh Jonno threw the ball to me, I missed it. and yep... it got me straight in the wedding tackle."

Wet as a shag on a rock
Soaked - drenched

"Howzit goin out there boys?"

"Mate it's pissin down, were as wet as a shag on a rock."

What will you do for a face when the monkey wants his arse back

Straight out of the Aussie sense of humour text book

"Hey Stevo, wadda ya gunna do for a face when the monkey wants his arse back."

"Oh yeh that's bloody hilarious dickhead."

He's not real bright

Where the crow flies backwards   Remote outback

"Iv'e hadda nough of this place Billy.
I'm off to where the crow flie backwards."

White pointers   Women's breast spotted on the beach

"Went down for a surf this mornin,
and spotted a couple of white pointers."

"Really waddja do."

"Well I kept lookin of course."

Who's cookin this chook   Who is in charge

"I know you've got an opinion,
but who's cookin this chook
me or you."

Woop Woop   Somewhere far away that no one knows

"Where the frigin hell is Wunurra?"

"It's in the middle of woop woop somewhere."

Wouldn't be dead for quids   Really happy to be alive

"Barney... How are ya, ya old bastard?"

"Mate I'm goin well, wouldn't be dead for quids."

Wouldn't shout if a shark bit im

"Rexy's next to shout drinks."　　　　Very tight with his money

"Mate good luck with that.
He wouldn't shout if a shark bit im."

Wouldn't that rip the fork out of ya nighty

　　　　　　　　　　　　　　　　Totally surprised

"Look at that Rexy did shout.
Wouldn't that rip the fork out of ya nighty."

Wouldn't touch it with a barge pole　　Not interested

"The deal sounded alright to me."

"Jonno if I was you mate,
I wouldn't touch it with a barge pole."

Wouldn't piss on im if he was on fire

I am not very found of this bloke

"He's a bloody low life,
I wouldn't piss on im if he was on fire."

Wouldn't read about it

Something unbelievable just happened

"Ya wouldn't read about it,
Jonno finally tied the knot."

Wouldn't have a bar of it

I am not getting myself involved with that

"Well I'll be buggered!
he wouldn't have a bar of it a few weeks ago,
but now he loves it."

Wrap your laughin gear round that

Please have something to eat

"There ya go Dazza,
I whipped ya up a feed.
Wrap ya laughin gear round that mate."

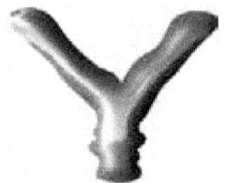

Ya bloods worth bottelin

Admiration for someone

"Ta mate, ya didn't have to fix that for us, Ya bloods worth bottlein."

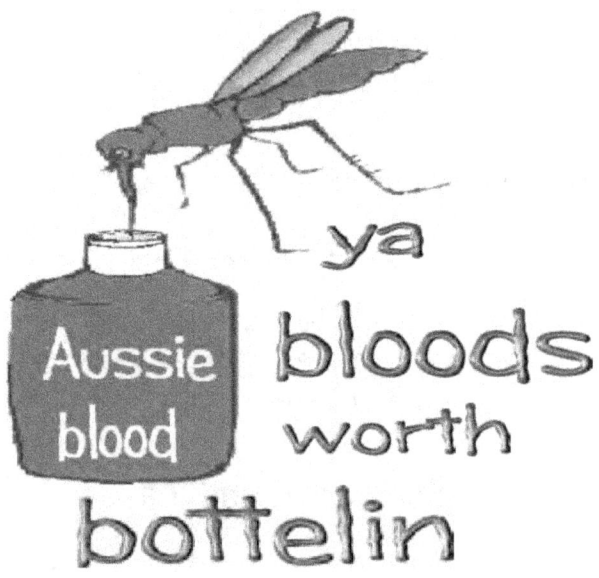

Ya bloody Wombat

You are such a silly person

"Don't twist it like that ya bloody wombat, give it here and I'll show ya how it's done."

Ya talkin shit mate   You are talking untrue my friend

"Watcha on about Johnsy,
ya talkin shit mate."

You bloody little pisser   To be pleased

"We finally had a win,
you bloody little pisser."

You must be the only living brain donor
     There is no intelligence

"You've gotta be kiddin me,
Why ja go and do that for?
fair dinkum,
you must be the only living brain donor."

You're a fruit cake   A bit mad, not quiet there

"Ya jumped off the city bridge,
you could've killed yourself,
you're a fruit cake mate."

You're a waste of sperm

Someone does not think highly of you

"Is that it...is that all you can think of to do all day. Watto sometimes I think you're a waste of sperm."

You're not wrong

You are correct

" That's pretty piss poor, don't ya reckon?"

"You're not wrong there."

Your eyes are bigger than your belly

Dined on a feast to his eyes liking not his stomach

"I'm as full as a goog, I think my eyes are bigger than my belly."

You've got buckleys

You have got no hope

"Bluey, you've got buckleys of catchin a fish, with that stupid lookin bloody rod of yours."

Zilch — Nothing

"Howja go Robbo,"

"No bloody good mate,
I got nothin,
zilch."

Zillion to one — An unimaginable huge amount

"Look I reckon the odds are against him a zillion to one,
he's got no hope."

---

flour
milk
a pinch of salt
and then
beat two eggs

So when you come across an Australian in ya travels
say "Gidday mate"
It'll give you a feeling of what it's like to be an Aussie

TM

Australians being Aussies

www.giddaymate.com.au